The Little Book of Spiritual Thoughts

"If we do not actively invest in our spiritual growth, quality of life remains shallow."

— Radhanath Swami

Illustrations by A.R. Lattimore

Copyright © 2021 by T.M Loftus-O'Leary
Cover design by A.R. Lattimore

All rights reserved. No part of this publication may be reproduced, distributed or transmitted in any form or by any means, including photocopying, recording or other electronic or mechanical methods, without the prior written permission of the author, except in the case of brief quotations embodied in reviews and certain other non-commercial uses permitted by copyright law.

Disclaimer: This book is designed to inspire in regards to the subject matter. It is sold with the understanding that the publisher and author are not rendering advise. The purpose of this book is to creatively encourage and entertain the reader. The author, publisher or distributors shall not be liable for any applications or actions performed by the purchaser.

The Emotional Guidance Scale referred to in this book
is from *Ask and It Is Given*, by Abraham Hicks

Printed in the United States of America
ISBN: 978-1-953910-85-1 (paperback)
ISBN: 978-1-953910-86-8 (ebook)

Canoe Tree Press

4697 Main Street
Manchester Center, VT 05255

Canoe Tree Press is a division of DartFrog Books.

Contact the Author:
https://loftusolearytm.wixsite.com/book
Email loftusolearytm@gmail.com
Facebook @loftusolearytm

Dedication

To Michael Francis Loftus

My brother Mike was a terrific guy generous, quick witted, handsome and extremely intelligent. Any grammatical errors I've made in this book would have come to his immediate attention. Mike, you left earth way too soon to soar, dance and sing with the angels. Your fun-loving spirit is sorely missed. Your family and friends keep fond memories of you in their hearts.

Acknowledgements

I wish to acknowledge and thank all those that have worked diligently and lovingly to make this place we call home better than which they found it. We all benefit from the Spiritual sensations that are felt when in the presence of an Enlightened heart.

A special thanks to my parents William and Loretta, my brother Michael, and my sisters Patricia and Catherine, for all your love and support. To my children Fawn, Lisa and Michael my love is always with you. To my grandchildren Garrett, Morgan, Olivia and Owen you have my heart. Lastly to my husband Robert who has let me freely and passionately express my Spiritual thoughts.

This book was helped along by my editor Loretta Loftus, my illustrator Andi Lattimore and the creative team at Canoe Tree Press.

Please enjoy your journaling experience
by writing, doodling and drawing your
thoughts and feelings on the
"My Expressions" pages.
Acknowledge your spiritual wisdom
by freely expressing your loving intentions.

Foreword

This book has been written over many years. My intention is to propose uplifting and positive ideas to incorporate into daily living. I hope some of the words lovingly motivate you to consciously create concepts leading to Self and Spiritual Awareness. You have the ability to generate loving thoughts. Certain matters may be out of your control but you can regulate your reactions by being mindful of an inspiring outcome. We all face frustrations, disappointments and sadness, but we can choose not to dwell worrisomely for long periods of time so as not to endanger our well-being. Concerning situations require you to be emotionally, mentally, physically and Spiritually present to obtain a peaceful resolve. Love, joy, happiness, peace and comfort naturally perpetuates pleasure. Spiritual fulfillment is calming and produces loving resolutions. As you slowly read each passage, contemplate each paragraph for a day or so before moving on to the next one. Quietly spend a few minutes exploring your loving thoughts, for Spiritual wisdom, then transfer your manifestations on to the journaling pages in the form of words, drawings and doodles. The repetitiveness of ideas is intentional to give slightly different ways of bringing Spiritual Enlightenment to your consciousness. Spirit, Creator, Source, Omnipotent, God are words, feelings and visions I use to appreciate that, that is indescribable.

Contents

Awakening 11
Start the Day on a Positive Note 13
Self-Love 15
Gratitude 17
Splendor 19
Contemplation 21
Vibrant Energy 23
Opportunity 25
Stillness 27
Grandeur 29
Trust 31
Beauty 33
Holiness 35
Being Present 37
Inner Peace 39
Self-Realization 41
Alignment 43
Change 45
You Are Divine 47
Inside Your Heart 49
Earth 51
Stuck 53
Optimism 55
Recognizing Fear 57
Practice Dedication and Courage 59
Overcome 61
Self-Awareness 63
Purpose 65
Letting Go of Negativity .. 67
Spiritual Connection 69
Spiritual Adventure 71
Spiritual Awareness 73
Spiritual Actions 75
Spiritual Energy 77
Spiritual Guidance 79
Spiritual Identification 81
Pursue Your Spiritual Nature 83
Spiritual Shift 85
Practicing Spirituality 87
Affirmations 89
Intuition 91
Joy-Filled 93
Healing 95
You Are Blessed 97
The End 99

Awakening

This is a very exciting time! As you awaken to Spiritual Energy you will be mystified by incredible tastes, sounds, colors and opportunities. Pursuit of gay possibilities is your vigorous heart set in motion by an unending belief in Spiritual Love. Gifting yourself with happy thoughts, forgiveness, gratitude and time for positive reflection opens your mind, heart and gut to Source. Inventing your trueness breaths hope into your ideas. When you experience the meaning of your life's purpose you will be stunned! It will be powerful! Certainly, something that you were not looking for will be revealed in a way that brings happiness into your heart.

My Expressions

Start the Day on a Positive Note

Entering fully into an awakened state of being takes a calm presence in your heart, body and mind. Awakening to Spirituality is felt in your heart and then brought to your senses through your thoughts. Seeing, feeling, hearing and touching grandeur is enjoyed when you open your heart to true love. Preparing for Spiritual guidance is clearing away blockages, such as fear, anger and resentments that are suppressed in your sub-conscious. Unfortunately, unresolved issues derail Spiritual Energy from creating exciting changes in your life. Low vibrational thinking fills your mind with negativity, that requires bright energy from inside your heart, to awaken positive well-being. Take time to prepare yourself for a blessed day by singing, listening to an uplifting message, walking in fresh air as you take several long deep breaths, praying, meditating, laughing, petting an animal, hugging someone or reading inspirational wisdom. A positive start of each day will help fend off negative reactions to situations that may occur. Let your true beauty lead you in reacting to your circumstances.

My Expressions

Self-Love

Self-esteem, from a Spiritual standpoint, is essential in gaining self-love. You encounter blame, spite, envy and anger from yourself and others when you do not have a precise understanding of your Spiritual significance. Divinity loves you beyond your recognition and that's all that matters. Take a trip inside your mind to vanquish buried pain so it no longer lingers to cause you hurt, worry and fear. Negative thoughts, that are suppressed, will continue to grow and produce reactions which may inadvertently pose health issues or damage relationships. Engaging in your own or someone else's pessimistic analyses of your self-worth is not productive. Forgiveness is necessary to conquer distress. Blame triggers resentment and fear that disrupts your Spiritual Awareness. Negative thoughts and actions do not fix a situation. Taking time to calm fearful thoughts will give Spiritual loving thoughts a chance to guide you through difficulties. Self-love activates you into action to overcome misconceptions your ego may have conjured up about yourself or others. In the presence of loving self-awareness, the ego is no longer in control to leave fear-based thoughts to fester and cause insecurity in your life. Moving forward progressively it is imperative to quietly contemplate your strengths to gain Spiritual Energy in your thoughts, your heart and your actions. Synchronicity of Spiritual and human thoughts and actions give birth to Spiritual Humanity.

My Expressions

Gratitude

Finding gratitude for the smallest of actions is your positive thoughts projecting joy into your life. Intention setting thoughts such as; I am happy, healthy, Spiritual, loving, grateful and prosperous, gives presence to your well-being. It will become second nature, to be completely grateful when you are presented gifts from nature and fellow beings, once you absorb Spiritual Energy. As you are treated to excited children, purring cats, vibrant flowers, singing birds, inspiring artists and puffy cloud formations, confront your inner Spirit which will lovingly connect your heart to these wonders. A walk outside, a glance through a window, watering a plant, laughing with a friend or petting an animal can release Spiritual Energy in your thoughts, heart and gut. Gratitude, innocence and love opens your eyes and your heart to the gifts of Creation. The pleasing observations that you pursue allows your mind, heart and soul to be steered by loving Spiritual Energy.

My Expressions

Splendor

Realization of true happiness is revealed as you witness silent soft flakes of snow falling from the sky. Take a few moments to contemplate their slow effortless descent, guided only by the wind, as they fall gracefully upon a tranquil evergreen. Spiritual splendor is the crystal flake adorning the evergreen branches. Open your heart to the magnificence of nature and become immersed in its splendor. Watch as the canvas is being painted by the unseen artist, and give your full attention to the exquisite beauty all around you.

My Expressions

Contemplation

The universe is infinite Spirit, intelligence, grace and love. All of this is inside of you as well as all around you. Spiritual contemplation provides an opportunity for consciousness to expand your queries as to why you are here on earth. Cognitive awareness of existence reaches beyond thoughts when Spiritual Awareness is present to your heart, gut and soul. In the silence of meditation and prayer Spiritual solutions become clear and rest in your consciousness. Spiritual mindfulness is a loving energy that changes perceptions of fear and hatred into forgiveness and gratitude. Your Spiritual Soul is so unimaginable that your unconscious ego is unable to believe in its existence. The ego does its best to build a blockade to impede your connection to Source. Thoughts, beliefs and actions should come from your heart, gut and soul to generate Spiritual outcomes. Being aware of the inner connection with Spiritual Energy can be brought to consciousness through self-awareness. Once love is restored in your heart your mind will no longer hold onto negativity. As the ego dissolves, self-esteem, self-awareness and self-love become manifested.

My Expressions

Vibrant Energy

You are surrounded by Spiritual Energy; it is inside of you, in nature, and in all other human beings. Resistance is working against the natural flow of Spiritual Energy and creates a low vibrational vacuum. Accepting and embracing high vibrant energy gives way to love, joy, peace and forgiveness. Like the descending snowflake there is nothing to be concerned with as you gently glide through space and time. Fear, anxiety and unforgiveness can block positive energy flow in your body, which in turn, prevents you from experiencing life from a passionate perspective. A conscious effort is needed to change your thoughts from anger to gladness. Spirit is available at all moments to guide you gently and peacefully on your journey. When Spiritual Energy seems to be absent, physically stop what you are doing, take a deep breath, smile, say a prayer, mantra or a memorized inspirational quote and let the peace you are generating guide your action. Activation of present moment positive energy will inspire greatness in your decision making.

My Expressions

Opportunity

Each day there is an opportunity for expansion in understanding Spiritual Awareness. Giving yourself a few minutes daily to relax and listen to your breath is a chance to revive your connection to Spiritual Energy. This cleansing and releasing process (mindfully breathing in a calming deep breath and releasing stress on the exhale) is a soothing way to clear your mind so you can enjoy your surroundings. Each morning and evening set aside time to get in tune with your Spirituality. Capture positive loving energy by silently contemplating your self-worth. Self-love gives your body, mind and soul the presence of everlasting peace and happiness. Any time is the right time to allow mindful, relaxing and peaceful breathes to preform present moment marvels. There is no right or wrong way to experience what the realization of self-awareness has to offer. Spiritual fulfillment is felt in your heart when you allow yourself a few minutes of serenity each day to contemplate your worthiness. A positive peaceful mind-set gives your Creator the opportunity to provide unimaginable wonders in your life.

My Expressions

Stillness

During the time you take to sit in prayer and meditation, keep an open mind so as to receive guidance from a higher Source. The soul awakens in the clarity that is created within stillness. The mind, the ego and distracting thoughts are met with non-resistance when in the quiet presence of Spirit. As you stay focused, on present moment awareness, it will allow interruptions to be acknowledged and then released as they pass through your conscious mind to be dissolved in your open heart. Realizing, the value of non-resistance will gently guide disturbances to fade out of your mind without contest. Let go easily of a negative thought by swapping it for a positive thought. Focusing on fearful thoughts interfere with your true Spiritual nature. Spiritual Energy will guide you to uncover love as you silence your fears, regrets and worries. Providing yourself with opportunities for silent resolve will have amazing effects on your mind, body and soul. There are many avenues to peacefulness. Be still, smile and be thankful for the Spiritual guidance you are given during your time of quiet meditative breathing. The route of following your heart instead of your head may seem unfamiliar, out of the way, and even weirdly wild, but faithfully following your inner wisdom is worth the ride.

My Expressions

Grandeur

Positive, happy, grateful, prosperous, healthy and gracious living is a choice. Joyful thoughts are present moment realisms as you, intentionally, seek Spiritual renewal. When you choose to engage your energy in loving and kind ways, negativity takes a backseat to happiness. When negative emotions try to do the driving, put on the brakes and maneuver in a positive direction. The journey of life spans a long distance, so give yourself time to see the sights. Flying down the road at top speed to get to the next destination may result in missed opportunities of enjoyment. The sunrises, sunsets, picnic lunches, singing birds, bright stars and laughter are clever ways Spirit is showing you love and happiness. You have a divine nature and incredible abilities to be explored as Spirit settles into your soul. Underneath the hood of subconsciousness stirs genius waiting to rev up your consciousness towards a positive passage. Grandeur lies beyond the barricade of unconscious suppressed fears. Shifting into reverse, to maneuver around unpleasant views only stalls your Spiritual progress. Undesirable baggage weighs down your thoughts which leads to decline. Cruising through doubt, worry and fear with Spiritual Love as the driver moves you forward into present moment realization of your divinity. Open up the map of Spiritual Awakening to find your destination. Travel light with love and happiness as your companions to prime your mind, heart and soul to experience true Spiritual ventures.

My Expressions

Trust

Nature offers many opportunities to unite with Spiritual Energy. Flowers, rivers, cardinals, snow, sun and trees all have an association with Spirit. Of course, any way you can connect to your Higher Self is wonderful. Reading, writing, drawing, painting, teaching, listening to music or whatever makes your heart sing is a link to loving energy. When Spiritual Energy is resisted you end up with perceived difficulties in your life. One form of resistance is trying to control every minute of your life. Regretting the past and worrying about the future is letting your egoic mind dictate outcomes. Trust that your heart, gut and mind have an inner connection with your Creator to guide and advise your thoughts and actions. Physically, emotionally and mentally stopping the inside chatter for several minutes a day to take in the outside foliage, clouds, rain, butterflies and flying falcons allows you to consciously appreciate Spiritual abundance. When you are in present moment awareness you are able to soak up everything creation has to offer. Managing your day becomes uninhibited as you trust, the inner heart felt Spiritual guidance keeping you on track, instead of relying on your steadfast mind.

My Expressions

Beauty

Encountering natural beauty reveals to your heart an eternal connection with Spirit. Spiritual realization urges wonderful adventures for your enjoyment. Aligning your life, with Spirit, guides your fascinating journey here on earth. Clarity of purpose is grasped as you contemplate the never-ending energy of the soul which connects with others and gives way to finding love. Love is Spiritual Energy that will impel you to soar above fear so you can feel, in your heart and soul, the workings of creation. Sustaining Spiritual Energy, which is not seen by the human eye yet felt in the unseen soul, blesses whatever you may be undergoing. Experiencing Spirituality leads you to releasing joy into your thoughts which invigorates positive energy into your actions. Your encounters will begin to reveal the true beauty of everyday existence when met with a positive open mind. Inner appreciation of nature is the grace of creation. Love is revealed in harmonious peacefulness as you unite with your Creator.

My Expressions

Holiness

Being aware of hope dwelling in your being sparks faith which encourages loving actions. Love is the intention of all creation. God and Jesus are the epitome of Love. Reaching for what you are intended to receive from Spirit takes faith and courage. Eliminating fearful thoughts is necessary to produce the outcome your Creator has in store for you. Holiness is reachable and ready to be tapped into, as you close your eyes and open your heart. Your desire for Spiritual Holiness to fill your heart does not go unnoticed by your Creator. There is an uniqueness in Spiritual Awakening that makes each individual seek clarity differently. The paths are many and more are in need of discovering to illuminate the journey to Spiritual realization. Parents, loved ones and friends may have a Spiritual journey to share with you but, ultimately, you must find your own path. Support is helpful but only you can give yourself the viable, peace, love and joy needed to grow Spiritually. The clergy, a spouse, co-workers, pets or children can witness a sacred shift in your life which is the result of your faith and trust in Spiritual Energy. As you undergo change, Self-love becomes evident. Positive energy is always available, when you seek it, to direct Spirit to bond with your heart, soul and mind. Mindfully speaking loving words, walking peacefully in nature and noticing your deep healing breath is to revel in Spiritual Energy.

My Expressions

Being Present

Unity with your Creator is achieved by surrendering the need to live life from past experiences and future uncertainties. Let go of the grip you have on worry, being anxious and the necessity to be in control. Releasing unease may sound very simple but, in reality, it is most difficult. Dwelling on past hurts and future burdens hinders the ever-present flow of Spiritual Energy. Present moment awareness is awakening to Spiritual Energy. The relationship you have with yourself and everything around you is defined by your awareness of being in the presence of Spiritual Love.

My Expressions

Inner Peace

Accepting the will of your Creator, and not your own, takes faith and unconditional self-love. Mentors can guide and help you but, ultimately, you have to take the steps of hope and faith so you can trust in your ability to grow in serenity. Searching for your sole journey to Spiritual Joy is a pursuit that is crucial for your inner peace. A great tool for relaxation and finding inner peace is meditation. Prayer, faith and hope complement the quest to finding Spiritual Energy. Silent contemplation, reading The Bible, writing, doing work you love, singing, running, laughing with friends or anything you feel a compassion for, is finding Spiritual Joy. Peace, love and joy are immensely quantified by allowing the Creator into your daily life. Revelations come from within as you realize the wonders Spiritual Energy is bringing you.

My Expressions

Self-Realization

Energy is constantly changing inside of you, and manifests opportunities for you to discern how to choose your thoughts and actions as either Spiritually or fearfully. Using your energy positively results in a pleasing outcome whereas negative energy allows anger, jealousy and hatred to dominate the situation. Each sunrise offers a new start with surprises to be unlocked. Self-realization of your Spirituality is all that is required for contentment. Fearfulness of the unknown leads to stagnation and will hinder the expansion of your life's purpose. Anxiety is worrying about what will happen in the future and results in fearful thoughts and actions. You do not want to rely on past experiences, that you considered failures, to stand in the way of your Spiritual growth. Giving the brain some well needed time off by sitting quietly, to experience heartfelt peace, is helpful in gaining Spiritual Enlightenment. As a whole, human experiences are moving in a Spiritual direction. Some beings are more accepting of shifting into Spiritual mode and others are unsure. Contemplating complete acceptance of your divine nature is a journey well-traveled. The love you give yourself will open up the awareness of your true nature. You cannot move into acceptance of being totally loved by your Creator until you completely love everything about yourself. Being happy as much as possible means you are on the right track of beautiful self-worthiness.

My Expressions

Alignment

Your body, mind and Spirit are intertwined with passionate joyous energy provided by your Creator and Source of Life. Realizing your connection to an Omnipotent Energy is the key to understanding gratitude, love, abundance, health, fulfillment and peace. When you are fully in the awareness of pure love your dreams and desires are present. Peace and love flow through your being when self-worth is recognized. Unforgiveness, resentments and envy have faint energy vibrations that stall your connection to pure love. Consciously letting go of guilt, anger and fear is necessary to restore self-esteem. Experiencing self-love every day is essential; look into a mirror and say out loud "I am truly wonderful"! Joy, peace and love will be evident once you have cleared the way to a state of self-acceptance. An awareness of being in a positive state of mind brings your dreams and desires in alignment with your life's higher purpose.

My Expressions

_____
_____
_____
_____
_____
_____
_____
_____
_____
_____
_____
_____
_____
_____
_____
_____

Change

To create positive change, in the present moment, is consciously releasing negative thoughts that have been steeped in your sub-conscious for years. When encountering an angry thought, take several long deep centering breaths. During the inhale your navel should expand and release during the exhale. As you concentrate on your breathing repeat to yourself, "I know only love and joy." Positive words and thoughts will free fearful thoughts to be dismissed out of your sub-consciousness. When faced with an aggravating situation, the natural negative reaction comes from a sub-conscious that is not kept in-check with present moment positive awareness. Positive Spiritual Energy is required to supersede angry negative thoughts. Fear and anger have been ingrained in our sub-conscious minds for generations. Disputes with loved ones, friends or co-workers happen when anger is not recognized as your defensive reaction. Peace, understanding of differences and forgiveness are healing responses that require conscious awareness to dissolve negative situations. Reconditioning your sub-conscious requires patience, self-awareness and present moment realization. Resolving a predicament is possible by not harshly reacting but being helpfully proactive in reconciling differences. Dislodging fear requires training your mind to treasure loving solutions. Having prepared yourself Spiritually with calming deep breaths, meditation and adapting self-love, will give you strength when faced with diversity. Attaining the ability to alter a negative situation into a positive one is life changing. When you are aware of your connection, with Spirit, fear cannot take control of you. The realization that you feel fear, but no longer need it to take hold of your thoughts, is Spiritual Awakening.

My Expressions

You Are Divine

Enjoyment, happiness and peace are thoughts that become experiences by a sense that is Godly Love. Seeing, hearing, touching, tasting and feeling are tangible senses that assist in happiness. Love is the underlining intangible sense occurring when Spiritual Awareness is present. The height of divinity is obtained when God Source Spirit become your heavenly reality on earth. Every situation is unique and has potential for exciting transcendence. Realization that you are divine is strongest when you are not experiencing fear or anger. Sensing Love, in every person and experience gives you strength to pursue your true Spiritual nature. You can soar, swim, dance, sit, build or write as you continue to grow Spiritually. Judgement confines your ability to create the unimaginable. Anticipating a fearful future or reliving the past causes worry and stifles creativity. When not aligned with Spiritual Awareness you may allow negative perceptions to determine a hopeless outcome of a situation. Give way to Spiritual Intelligence to provide understanding to your activities. Experiencing a circumstance or event Spiritually provides understanding that there is a loving way to resolution. Preconceiving an event as good or bad can hinder your understanding of Spiritual insights that are available to give you unworldly growth. Trying to intellectually understand what the reasoning is behind a seemingly unfortunate circumstance will only hold you in a state of frustration. Having a relationship with yourself and others that continue to produce thoughts and actions using negative emotions will keep you from your divine nature and put you at risk for more sadness and fear. Give Spirit a shot at partnering up with you to keep your quarrels positive and your thoughts pure and loving.

My Expressions

Inside Your Heart

When will the problems stop showing up? When will anger and fear stop being a reaction to circumstances? Life is always in flux and there are accidents, disagreements, death, divorce etc... Reacting negatively to what you can or cannot control is being unaware of your Spiritual strengths. To keep balanced, silently or out loud, ask Spirit to help you open your heart, mind and soul to effectively sustain positive understanding. Acknowledging Spirit as the handler of your life takes practice, patience, faith, prayer and meditative time to accept. Changing your thought process is necessary to developing a loving peaceful relationship with family members, co-workers, the environment and especially yourself. You are responsible for how you react and feel inside your heart. The brilliance of an Omnipotent Intelligence, in and around you that is strengthening your heart and guiding you to happiness, is just a mindset away. Giving yourself the opportunity to enjoy the outcome of a loving mind and heart will spill out into your relationships and your life in general.

My Expressions

Earth

Taking care of your well-being, your emotions, your thoughts, your actions and your body is necessary to serve others and the planet in a positive way. As an individual, becoming aware of your true nature allows your eyes to open to the delicatessen of life. Perceiving through your heart and gut will uncover great treasures that will expand your understanding of Spirituality. Believing in yourself creates the self-worth, self-esteem and self-love needed to pursue healing in others and the earth. To love yourself, others and the planet is Spiritually Self-Serving. Spiritual Awareness guides you to appreciating, caring for and nurturing the universe.

My Expressions

Stuck

Next time that you are stuck in traffic, a boring meeting or a grocery store line, say a prayer. Bless yourself for having patience while you wait your turn. Your spouse, co-worker or even a stranger will appreciate your loving attitude. Look not to what may be going wrong, in your eyes, but look to see something hopeful in every situation. Randomly, bless everyone you can think of without exclusions. Reconnect yourself to happy thoughts by reciting a poem, singing a song or reading a beloved Scripture. Look for the goodness and overlook the rudeness. Negative circumstances can be used as a lesson to step up to the next level of true happiness and joy on your exciting journey. Every situation is an opportunity for Spiritual growth. As you practice patience and forgiveness, true happiness will frequent your heart and mind.

My Expressions

Optimism

The Divine Creator is patiently waiting for you to follow your heart to the kingdom. Take time to listen to your inner voice for gentle guidance. If there is doubt about anything, and there will be doubt, don't blame anyone, especially yourself, for bewildering thoughts. Stop the confusion and worry as soon as you realize the appearance of negativity. Move past the disappointment to hopefulness and be optimistic. Take a few minutes each day to think of one or two things in your life to be grateful for. Gratitude influences your thoughts in a positive way. Bring joy into your life by letting go of unease and focusing on your heart inspired reality. Resisting your Spiritual nature gums up the flow of positive thoughts. A wonderous joyfulness is inside of you ready to replace anger and fear. Blockages that are caused by grief, hatred and worry will dissipate as you concentrate on accepting the flow of Spiritual Energy throughout your entire body. Gaining access to a resting place within your divine nature starts from within by eliminating fear-based thoughts so you can lie in peace. The pathway to heaven on earth radiates with love and all will join into the glow together.

My Expressions

Recognizing Fear

The effortless flow of the environment offers many opportunities to resonate with your Spiritual Energy. Being in-tune with your inner voice, listening to others as they speak, and observing nature are ways that connect you to Spirit. Negative interference causes resistance and you lose your connection with inner joy. The result of resisting Spiritual Energy can cause complexities in your life. Recognizing that fear and anger have entered into your mind and heart is the first step in replacing negative behavior with positive actions. Thoughts are clever as they embed worry, envy and sadness into your subconscious, this negativity can spread quickly to your actions if not kept in check. As situations arise, Be Aware that consciously allowing past negative thoughts to dominate the emotions of your present state of being is possible. Thinking on auto-pilot renders sad emotions to surface, that originated from past hurts, which can affect a present moment situation. You are being serviced by your past experiences when you are unaware of your Spiritual ability to tackle a concern. Tending to over-compensate for a lack of control, over present moment consciousness, turns into desperately trying to regulate the future. Changing your reality to be Fully Aware in the present moment is possible by asking your Creator for guidance. Realizing there are peaceful options in every circumstance gives you Spiritual strength to carry on.

My Expressions

Practice Dedication and Courage

Conceptions about what you are experiencing at the present moment should come from a place of love. Practicing a joyful nature is a lesson well-worth learning. Self-love and positive awareness are key in fundamentally awaking to thoughts of happiness, peacefulness, abundance and joy. Begin to believe that you can make positive changes in your life with the help of Spiritual Energy. Wonderful inspiring affirmations are commendable for Spiritual growth. Dedication and courage will overcome the resistance to stay stuck in the past. A commitment to become self-aware, in the present moment, is the start of non-resistance. Vulnerability seeps into your thoughts when you knowingly stop trying to control the future and let go of the past. As you relinquish self-doubt to Spiritual guidance an uneasy feeling of helplessness may occur. Once you understand the significance of giving your will to Spirit you overcome fear and become rejuvenated. Obtaining true happiness is experienced when you accept your Creator as the Source of unconditional Love. Unification with Spirit is realized when you pray and meditate. Spiritual Awakening develops in a quiet place within your mind as you close your eyes, breathe deeply and clear out all distractions. Simply by not trying to direct the future you begin to live in the present moment and that is a wonderful step in Spiritual growth. Present moment awareness becomes a new way of life when realization that the old ways of thinking are slowing your Spiritual development. Abandoning your old thought patterns and living in the present moment of self-awareness and self-love is the game changer in your Spiritual Enlightenment.

My Expressions

Overcome

Experiencing life from a joyful perspective sounds easy. So why does it take such an effort for happiness to take hold of your thoughts? Your quest to seek joy is obstructed by fearful thoughts about yourself, others and your Creator. Inevitably it takes patience, forgiveness and faith to experience joy. Changing your outlook on how to process anger, fear and resentment is necessary to experience joy, and can be done in a multitude of ways. One way is stepping mindfully into a high vibrational energy by releasing your fears and turning them first into disappointments, then into frustration, then into hopefulness and ultimately into happiness. These are stepping stones used in an Emotional Guidance Scale developed by Abraham Hicks to mindfully overcome negativity. Reading some great inspirational books, meditation, walking in nature, deep breathing and prayers are positive actions that lessen worry, blame and anger. Practice engaging in a positive distraction such as; a walk around the block, petting an animal, taking a warm bath or enjoying a cup of tea when you are faced with diversity. Think of your favorite things in life while taking several deep breaths, envisioning yourself on a beach relaxing on a hammock or any joy-filled thought that will keep you positive on your journey. Spiritual guidance is always with you when you sit silently and let your breath take you to a deeper part of yourself. Present moment awareness that you are a person of interest in your blessed body, mind and soul will guide you to find Spiritual strength to overcome sadness.

My Expressions

Self-Awareness

Self-Awareness is necessary to achieve Spiritual Enlightenment and attain a joy-filled day. Procuring a positive thought while encountering a crisis is connecting with your inner beauty as you perform optimistically in the present moment. Coming to terms with your self-worth is essential to achieving Spiritual changes in your life. Comprehending Spiritual-Awareness takes practice, self-understanding and patience. The more you practice Spiritual and self-awareness the less amount of time it takes to recover from a blow you were not expecting. The process used to move past the anger of an experience, individual or group of individuals, to a place of dignity, takes courage. Have faith that you are strong enough to change your anger into peace. Eventually, the hurts and disappointments will not be a source of negativity once you are content within yourself, instead they will be a resource for Spiritual growth. Having a firm grasp of the importance of knowing your self-worth moves you into a spectacular space. You will realize a transformation from anger, fear, resentment and guilt to love, appreciation, joy and excitement as you are strengthened by Spiritual self-worth. The blossoming to true Spiritual-Awakening in your life will take off as you decide to open up to unlimited possibilities.

My Expressions

Purpose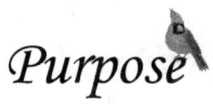

Your Spiritual Soul is so unimaginable that your uncomprehending intellect stands in the way of the energy that connects you to your purpose. Your purpose will be found through actions directly resulting from Spiritual consciousness. Thoughts and beliefs are meant to come from your Spiritual soul. Negative thoughts can misguide you. When you have not fully forgiven yourself, of mistakes you think you have made, you cycle in a downward spiral. Giving yourself the opportunity to forgive, will let in the light of your soul that, leads you in positive decision making. Once the negative thoughts have been dispelled, your divine purpose can blossom. Joy in discovering your role results from your conscious union with your Spiritual soul.

My Expressions

Letting Go of Negativity

Your true joy-filled journey is experienced when you let go of your negative and fearful thoughts and enter the realm of peacefulness. Negative thoughts, which are not from your Spirit, but found in the ego, bring you to the path of resistance which is a long, bumpy, treacherous road. Intellectual thoughts of control and obtaining the upper hand come from worry and fear. Gloomy thoughts, that have not yet been released from your body and mind, control the actions you take especially in difficult situations. Until you release harmful thoughts from your sub-conscious, you continue to fear what should not be fearful. Fear constitutes protection from rivals, resentment causes jealous reactions, and judgements produce vengeance. Overall irritation and the negativity that it produces accumulates in your egocentric mind. Once you pinpoint the situation that is causing your anger, it can be dissolved so it does not continue to run havoc inside your thoughts. Each day presents the chance to keep the ego in check so you can enjoy Spiritual Energy moving throughout your mind and body. Deep relaxing, releasing breaths begin to bring awareness to your strengths. Your heart will develop a Spiritual belief which overrides bogus situations that enter into your life. The Awareness of not giving-in to a pretentious circumstance is healing. Being conscious of the connection to your inner Spiritual light gives you the capability to walk through a darkened path. Meditating on the gifts in your life allows gratitude to entertain your thoughts and push away sorrow.

My Expressions

Spiritual Connection

As you allow yourself time to unite with the unending flow of Spiritual Energy, your journey swells with joyous experiences. Spiritual encounters can appear as a chance meeting with friends, relatives or strangers, articles or books, animals or any unforeseen opportunity that seems to pop-up as a sign of your divine connectedness to Spirit. Prosperity, health and happiness replace despair, hurt and anger as Spiritual thoughts are brought into focus. Having an awareness that you are worthy of receiving wonderful gifts for just being yourself propels profound experiences to transform your life. Your mind, body and Spiritual connection provides energy that is always available and keeps you in-tune with your highest purpose in life. Linking your mind, heart and gut is obtained when you are aware of how, relaxed, happy, inspired and fulfilled you feel. Meditation and prayer will be profoundly enhanced as conscious, present moment inner awareness, silences the gibberish of your mind and touches your heart.

My Expressions

Spiritual Adventure

Spiritual adventure is experiencing an exuberant life through an open heart. By exploring the transition of fearful negative thoughts to positive loving ones elevates you from low energy to a high voltage lifestyle. The true nature of your being is allowing Spiritual Energy to captivate your mind, body and soul. It is in the present moment where all Spiritual Energy is concentrated and yields happiness, excitement and adventure. Acceptance that there is a Spiritual purpose in your life is needed to understand your worthiness. Acknowledging Spiritual Energy, as your guide on this wonderous journey you are having on earth, is stepping into truth. Close your eyes and intuitively open your heart to Source, which is unimaginably delightful and, will lead you on your travels.

My Expressions

Spiritual Awareness

Relinquishing cognitive control for Spiritual Awareness allows you to speak from the heart not the head. The logical thinking that keeps you stuck in your anger is ego driven. Taking a leap of faith is needed to change fearful thoughts to loving ones. Transitioning from fear to love is an adventure that awakens the Spirit within you. Every day give yourself time to take some very deep breaths to prepare you for meditation and prayer. There are numerous references including books, videos and classes you can access to help with the process of relaxation and mindful thinking, which in turn will allow Spiritual Energy to guide you. A renewed heart-felt energy will immerge when accepting Spirit inside your being. Positive thoughts generated by your Spiritual mindfulness will block thoughts of fear and keep you on track for a brilliant day.

My Expressions

Spiritual Actions

Your Spiritual progress accelerates when you are mindfully staying positive while experiencing trying situations. The goal is to become self-aware so you can consciously dismiss the "trigger point" that alters your calm happy state of mind to becoming frustrated. You can stop an action, that is driven by anger, by choosing a positive action driven by Spiritual Energy. Reflecting on receiving guidance from your higher self deflects lower vibrational thoughts of fear and anger. Negative thoughts, that would normally develop into vengeful actions, will become fewer and fewer when concentrating on trusting your Creator for help. Being mindful and present when resolving negative situations is an opportunity for Spiritual growth. Trust and faith in Spiritual resolutions for your concerns is powerful. Being aware of negative thoughts as soon as they arise allows you to pursue positive outcomes using Spiritual mindfulness. Your responses to everyday situations can be observed by an inner state of Spiritual peacefulness. A high vibrational connection to Spiritual Energy, is the result of your conscious efforts of being mindful of the circumstances you are faced with. Present moment self-awareness lovingly creates Spiritual actions.

My Expressions

Spiritual Energy

The True Nature of your physical Being is allowing Spiritual Energy to encapsulate your thoughts and your body. Spirituality is timeless, effortless and is your truest, purest self. Spirituality is the dimension where your Soul presides and not your conscious thoughts. Here in a higher dimension your physical body, mind and Spirit become rejuvenated. Life, in union with creation, is allowing yourself to be in the hands of your Creator. Relinquishing resistance to know your omnipresent self, the awakened self, will result in an awareness of the almighty power and presence of your Creator. That which knows only love, which does not judge, that which is infinite unconditional appreciation of all life forms is part of you. As you allow Spiritual Energy to enter your everyday life, you become fully present. This presence allows you to be joyful, grateful and blessed. All the treasures the universe offers; plants, water, animals, the sky, wind and air, gives you opportunities to look inward to your true nature. Spiritual self-awareness allows your mind, body and emotions to appreciate what is surrounding you. We are blessed by Creation. Willingness to be happy where you stand gives enjoyment and access to everything Spirit has to offer you.

My Expressions

Spiritual Guidance

Believing in a Spiritual Energy that provides means to unknot your sails is enlightening. Once your conscious mind realizes that the loving presence of your inner Spirit is able to handle the most precarious situations, your doubts, worries and grievances unravel. Worry is reduced as you realize your life is in good hands. Blame and resentment, that resulted from past experiences, can be replaced with compassion and gratitude when inner peace is realized. Present moment challenges give you a chance to respond Spiritually or egotistically. There is a lesson and a growth opportunity every time you use Spiritual understanding to clear up a negative state of affairs. Spiritual Awareness occurs when you realize that your intellectual ways of handling fear and doubt can be replaced with love. Fear represents blockages that keep your conscious thoughts from receiving divine guidance generated by Spirit. The absence of negative thoughts is critical to your Spiritual Enlightenment. Choosing happy, positive, loving thoughts over anger, blame and fear removes blockages and invites Spiritual Energy to handle present moment resolutions. As you practice present moment awareness the skies clear and Spiritual hands gently navigate your journey.

My Expressions

Spiritual Identification

Earth is a Spiritual Place. You are a Spiritual Being. Your life is a Spiritual Journey. Amen. You have opportunities to connect with all that is. Your Higher Spiritual Self is truly amazing. Self-realization is knowing you ARE an amazing Being. Present moment Spiritual Awareness is self-awareness. Connecting Spiritual Energy to your present moment circumstance is positive self-awareness bringing forth inner peace and love. Learning to become self-aware takes patience and the undoing of perceived difficulties. Over-coming harsh, self-defeating thoughts clear the way for fresh, kind and loving thoughts to be your natural way of dealing with life. Past negative thoughts put you at a disadvantage, by giving you low energy, restricting your Spiritual growth. Future intentions to control outcomes can be very disappointing when wishes become unfulfilled. Spiritual Awareness is the tool needed to guide you to understanding that your thoughts have the ability to pursue a positive outcome when facing fearful situations. Opening your heart to Spiritual Energy, given out of love from Creation, is all powerful and renewing. Intentionally gravitating to a loving outcome, from an outward worrisome situation, is a powerful Spiritual choice. You are equipped with everything needed on your earthly journey to identify with your Spiritual Self.

My Expressions

Pursue Your Spiritual Nature

Sitting quietly and breathing purposefully creates an atmosphere of peace and calm which stimulates your mind to obtain sincerity. Answers to your questions, concerns and prayers silently appear in your serene mind when engaged in Spiritual Awareness. The peace and love of Spiritual Energy will fill your mind, heart and body, during times of disorder, when you become aware of the high vibrational power awareness provides. Pursue awareness of Spiritual guidance by quieting the mind with prayer, yoga, a run, soothing sounds, meditation, a mantra or a silent walk in nature. As your mind loosens its grip on negativity your heart will fill with positive ways to stay in present moment peace. The pursuit of peaceful answers is just as valuable as the answers themselves. To hear options to your queries, stop, smile, laugh, be happy, and then listen with your heart and gut as Spirit provides answers. Keep your heart and mind open to sighting the moon in the middle of the day, a rainbow, a gentle breeze or an unexpected resource to wander into your life. Do not dismiss an offering from Spirit.

My Expressions

Spiritual Shift

As you begin to surrender your fearful and worrisome thoughts recognition of Spiritual Energy occurs. Leaping into the unknown territory of Spiritual realization will transform your heart and mind into a state of pure love. Inner Spiritual Awareness dissolves negativity and inspires loving positive thoughts and actions. Allow the awareness of your Spirituality to shine into the outer world to dissolve uncertainties. Circumstances you have no control over are being dealt with by the Almighty Creator. When you notice you are reacting negatively to issues, in or beyond your control, it's imperative to surrender fear, anger and blame to love. As you shift gears from low powered negative thoughts to high powered loving thoughts, you will gain momentum in the pursuit of Spiritual tendencies.

My Expressions

Practicing Spirituality

Now is a perfect time to acknowledge the Spiritual Energy that is inside of you and all around you. The key is to keep your thoughts in good Spirits. When there is negative chatter going on, the sooner you become aware of it, the easier it will be to stop. Self-awareness is the recognition of annoying thoughts and the realization that there are loving and graceful thoughts available as replacements. Choosing to love, to be happy and to forgive replaces fear, anger and worry. Verse wonderous thoughtful aims anytime you want to spread love, peace and joy. Affirmations such as, "I am patient, kind and forgiving", "I am filled with peace and love" or "I am strong, healthy, talented, abundant and happy", can kick start your acceptance of self-love so you can spread cheer to others. As you tie in your practice with everyday life you will feel Spiritual Energy wherever you may be. Optimistic thoughts materialize without much help from your consciousness, and you will see a delightful change in your Spirit.

My Expressions

Affirmations

Using Affirmations throughout the day gives you time to reflect on your worthiness and your connection to Creation. Meditation, yoga and mindful walking can be incorporated with affirmations as you silently, or out loud, acknowledge how wonderful, beautiful and talented you are. The realization that you are the Creator's fulfillment of, love, kindness, helpfulness and joy is you giving life to Spiritual Awakening. Your thoughts, words and actions give way to living a life of profound Spiritual intimacy. The tendency to seek higher ground when confronted with unworthy thoughts, about yourself or others, will lift you to new heights of Spiritual understanding. Uplifting words will give support when you encounter a negative situation because affirmations, meditation and prayer will keep you in a conscious state of Spiritual Awareness. The guidance you receive when awakened to an Omnipresent Source is invaluable to your happiness and well-being. Obtaining a vision of virtue becomes clear when you uphold a silent loving Creator standing by your side. Glimpses of beauty immerge as your mind and heart gaze out at the wonders of creation. Affirmations such as; "I am surrounded by diverse beauty" or "I am open to receiving all creation has to offer me on this glorious day," keeps you in sync with Spiritual Energy.

My Expressions

Intuition

A dynamic energy is felt when you are able to enjoy your Spiritual intuition. Undeniably having faith in an energy greater than you can imagine that is always available to provide answers goes beyond reasoning. Spiritual Energy which is unidentifiable using your eyes and ears, cannot be explained in rational terms but is intuitively felt in your heart and gut. A sense, that is beyond what is cognitively used to understanding universal nature, is available when you rely on Spiritual Energy. The complicated universe holds many unanswered questions. Cognitive thoughts joined together with Spiritual intuition loving resolves physical world situations. Choosing positive thoughts places you at a high energy level where Spiritual readiness dwells. Negative thoughts cause low energy levels where reactive ego making decisions occur. Jesus, prophets, philosophers, poets, Enlightened Spiritual Beings suggest placing your thoughts in a loving, forgiving, joy-filled state, rising your Spiritual intuition, which creates a higher understanding of life.

My Expressions

Joy-Filled

Positive thoughts, which are Spiritual by nature, seek a way to bring joy into your present moment awareness. Giving Spirit a chance to interact in your daily activities activates a loving atmosphere. Little effort is needed from your ego to enjoy bliss. Any second thoughts or after thoughts as to why happiness is always showing up will be washed away when ego is put to rest. You will continue to be enlightened as you make room in your mind for joy-filled thoughts. A shift is bound to occur and Spiritual Awareness will begin to heal you when negative thoughts are released. Fear of failure prevents you from leaving behind what has become the norm to living a joy-filled life. Failure is not an option and your intended purpose is always within reach. You are a Spiritual Being finding your way around in the universe. The higher your Spiritual Energy is vibrating the more you feel the love, joy and peace inside of you and around you.

My Expressions

Healing

Coming out of an angry state and into a state of happiness involves present moment self-awareness. Adjusting your state of mind from lack and fear to abundance and love requires mindfully practicing patience, forgiveness, gratitude and opening your heart to Spiritual Energy. Fear, anger and resentment are activated in your subconscious through the door of past negative experiences which can wreak havoc in the present moment. Unconsciously, stirring negative thoughts around in your head creates a vortex of fear. Consciously placing anxiety, distress and self-blame into your heart, as you forgive yourself and others, will dissolve the hurt of past issues. To get negativity out of your head, to be healed in your heart, you should stop what you are doing and rub your palms together for several seconds, then place your hands on your heart. Concentrating on your inhale, breath in deeply while saying, "I love myself". On the exhale say, "I'm releasing all negativity from my body". Also, lightly tapping your forehead between your eyebrows and saying, "I am healed, healthy, happy and open to Spiritual guidance", is a great way to activate positive self-awareness. These techniques, along with other Spiritually awakening thoughts and activities, give you an opportunity to smile and purposefully grant yourself time to heal. Spiritual vigor shines light into dark troubles, rejuvenating sacred self-worth to restore healing. Enthusiastically bonding with Creation livens your Spirit consciousness as it soars to new heights. With blockages gone, Spiritual Energy sets forth loving and peaceful thoughts into your present moment awareness.

My Expressions

You Are Blessed

Engaging peacefully in your surroundings is tapping into Spiritual Energy that is waiting to be of service. Become aware of peacefulness by appreciating the wonderful people, animals and objects near you or in your heart. Intercept the Spiritual Energy all around you so it can guide you to a blessed state of being. As Spiritual Energy surrounds you, become aware that you are intertwined with Creation. The creative plan that Creation envisioned for you is beyond description. A design created from love, that is ever-changing and, when you are mindful of it, will illustrate answers you are seeking. Fear of modifying your life is an unnecessary discord that holds you back from love, peace and joy. A Spiritual shift starts the gears of your mind, heart, gut and soul to powerfully move you in a divine direction. Your egotistical perception of circumstances should not dictate how much happiness you encounter during your day, the discovery of Spirit should. Awareness of a loving Spiritual Energy will guide you to experiencing your joyful nature. Realization that Spirit is silently at work putting all the pieces of your life together is a grand blessing.

My Expressions

The End

A Spiritual life style is choosing to make decisions with your heart. Your thoughts will expand when awareness is given room to connect you to your Creator. As your mind, body, soul and Spirit unite, you will enjoy the love, peace and joy awakening brings. May mature radiance fill your thoughts and produce actions of gratitude, patience, kindness and love as it spreads to others. As humanity continues to grow Spiritually, the continued appreciation of relationships, the earth, mistakes, opportunities, and knowledge unite us. Love, forgiveness and positive thoughts are always an option when faced with concerns. Giving yourself permission to be present, as Creation spills forth wonders, is a life filled with Spiritual Enlightenment.

My Expressions

"When I look at the heavens, the work of your fingers, the moon and the stars that you have established; what are human beings that you are mindful of them, mortals that you care for them? Yet you have made them a little lower than angels and crowned them with glory and honor. You have given them dominion over the works of your hands; you have put all things under their feet, all sheep and oxen, and also the beasts of the field, the birds of the air, and the fish of the seas, whatever passes along the paths of the seas. O Lord our Sovereign, how majestic is your name in all the earth!"
—Psalm 8:3-9 (NRSV)

My Expressions

"Do not judge, and you will not be judged; do not condemn, and you will not be condemned. Forgive, and you will be forgiven; give, and it will be given to you."
—Luke 6:37-38 (NRSV)

My Expressions

"Loving others is easy when I love and accept myself"

"The more peaceful I am inside the more peace I have to share"

"I act as if I already have what I want—it's an excellent way to attract happiness in my life."

"I now live in limitless love, light and joy."
—Louise Hay

My Expressions

"Whatever arises…love that"

"The true benchmark of spiritual maturity is how often your words and actions are aligned with love."

"Sincerity is the willingness to accept how beautiful you already are. In such beauty, all is embraced and everything is included."

"You cannot doubt yourself, and enjoy yourself at the same time. Therefore, free yourself of doubt, by enjoying yourself in all that you do."
—Matt Kahn

My Expressions

About the Author

Theresa O'Leary lives a few miles from the shores of South Carolina. She spends her time gardening, walking, collecting beach trinkets and golfing amongst other things. Thoughtful discussions with family and friends are always spirited and lively. Yoga, Pilates, reading, praying and meditating are daily practices that keeps her in the here and now. Theresa is thankful every day for all that comes her way!

www.ingramcontent.com/pod-product-compliance
Lightning Source LLC
Chambersburg PA
CBHW071421070526
44578CB00003B/643